Greater Thai
Reviews from Readers

I think the series is wonderful and beneficial for tourists to get information before visiting the city.

-Seckin Zumbul, Izmir Turkey

I am a world traveler who has read many trip guides but this one really made a difference for me. I would call it a heartfelt creation of a local guide expert instead of just a guide.

-Susy, Isla Holbox, Mexico

New to the area like me, this is a must have!

-Joe, Bloomington, USA

This is a good series that gets down to it when looking for things to do at your destination without having to read a novel for just a few ideas.

-Rachel, Monterey, USA

Good information to have to plan my trip to this destination.

-Pennie Farrell, Mexico

Great ideas for a port day.

-Mary Martin USA

Leira Matubis

Aptly titled, you won't just be a tourist after reading this book. You'll be greater than a tourist!

-Alan Warner, Grand Rapids, USA

Thank you for a fantastic book.

-Don, Philadelphia, USA

Even though I only have three days to spend in San Miguel in an upcoming visit, I will use the author's suggestions to guide some of my time there. An easy read - with chapters named to guide me in directions I want to go.

-Robert Catapano, USA

Great insights from a local perspective! Useful information and a very good value!

-Sarah, USA

This series provides an in-depth experience through the eyes of a local. Reading these series will help you to travel the city in with confidence and it'll make your journey a unique one.

-Andrew Teoh, Ipoh, Malaysia

>TOURIST

GREATER THAN A TOURIST – NAGOYA CITY AICHI PREFECTURE JAPAN

50 Travel Tips from a Local

Leira Matubis

Leira Matubis

Greater Than a Tourist- Nagoya City Aichi Prefecture Japan Copyright © 2018 by CZYK Publishing LLC. All Rights Reserved.

All rights reserved. No part of this book may be reproduced in any form or by any electronic or mechanical means including information storage and retrieval systems, without permission in writing from the author. The only exception is by a reviewer, who may quote short excerpts in a review.

Cover designed by:
Cover Image:

Greater Than a Tourist
Visit our website at www.GreaterThanaTourist.com

Lock Haven, PA
All rights reserved.
ISBN: 9781980760771

>TOURIST

50 TRAVEL TIPS FROM A LOCAL

Leira Matubis

>TOURIST

BOOK DESCRIPTION

Are you excited about planning your next trip?

Do you want to try something new?

Would you like some guidance from a local?

If you answered yes to any of these questions, then this Greater Than a Tourist book is for you.

Greater Than a Tourist- Nagoya City Aichi Prefecture Japan by Leira Matubis offers the inside scoop on Nagoya City. Most travel books tell you how to travel like a tourist. Although there is nothing wrong with that, as part of the Greater Than a Tourist series, this book will give you travel tips from someone who has lived at your next travel destination.

In these pages, you will discover advice that will help you throughout your stay. This book will not tell you exact addresses or store hours but instead will give you excitement and knowledge from a local that you may not find in other smaller print travel books.

Travel like a local. Slow down, stay in one place, and get to know the people and the culture. By the time you finish this book, you will be eager and prepared to travel to your next destination.

Leira Matubis

>TOURIST

TABLE OF CONTENTS

BOOK DESCRIPTION
TABLE OF CONTENTS
DEDICATION
ABOUT THE AUTHOR
HOW TO USE THIS BOOK
FROM THE PUBLISHER
OUR STORY
WELCOME TO
> TOURIST
INTRODUCTION
1. ENTER THROUGH NAGOYA
2. STAY IN NAGOYA
3. AVOID AUGUST
4. KAKIGORI
5. THE GRAND SUMO TOURNAMENT
6. FIREWORKS FESTIVALS
7. HIGASHI BETSUIN TEMPLE
8. SUBWAYS & RAILS
9. THE RAIL / SKYBUS
10. FRUIT PICKING AT TOGOKUSAN
11. TOKUGAWA ART MUSEUM

Leira Matubis

12. NAGOYA CASTLE
13. STONE WALLS
14. THE KINSHACHI
15. 400-YEAR OLD SAMURAI
16. THE NAMELESS THEATRE
17. KABUKI CAFE
18. OSU SHOPPING
19. FEED THE PIGEONS
20. ISE SHRINE
21. ATSUTA SHRINE
22. SHIROTORI GARDEN
23. VISIT AT NIGHT
24. THE NEST
25. THE ROCK
26. SHOOTERS
27. NAGOYA CITY SCIENCE MUSEUM
28. HIGASHIYAMA ZOO
29. TOYOTA COMMEMORATIVE MUSEUM
30. NORITAKE GARDEN
31. TASTE FRESH BEER
32. BEER GARDENS
33. NAGOYA SOUL FOOD
34. FOOD FROM THE BASEMENT
35. NAGASHIMA SPALAND
36. STEEL DRAGON

>TOURIST

37. WHITE CYCLONE
38. JAZZ DREAM
39. NABANA NO SATO
40. WINTER ILLUMINATION
41. YUAMI NO SHIMA
42. NAGOYA SWEETS AND SNACKS
43. FLUFFY PANCAKES
44. CURRY PAN
45. ROUND ONE AND SPOCHA
46. PORT OF NAGOYA PUBLIC AQUARIUM
47. LEGOLAND
48. SCMAGLEV AND RAILWAY PARK
49. NAGOYA SOUVENIRS
50. OTHER SPOTS AND NEIGHBORING PLACES
TOP REASONS TO BOOK THIS TRIP
50 THINGS TO KNOW ABOUT PACKING LIGHT FOR TRAVEL
> TOURIST
GREATER THAN A TOURIST
> TOURIST
GREATER THAN A TOURIST
NOTES

DEDICATION

This book is dedicated to my boyfriend, the primary reason why Nagoya is my home. Without whom, I would never be in the city I've learned to love.

Leira Matubis

ABOUT THE AUTHOR

Leira is an English teacher who has lived in Nagoya since 2016. She moved to Japan to live with her long-time boyfriend after 2 years of a gruelling long-distance relationship. Leira is originally from the Philippines, a country known for captivating nature, numerous islands and a ridiculous number of texts.

Leira was not born a traveler unlike the other women in her family. Her mother would constantly be traveling Southeast Asia while her sister regularly explored domestic gems. She, however, opted for the comfort of their home but on the infrequent occasion that she traveled, it was in the insistence of someone else.

Nagoya is her first international travel experience. She first visited her boyfriend's hometown back in 2015. Although she stayed in Nagoya, sightseeing and weekend trips were done in other tourist locations in Japan.

After a few other similar visits, Leira relocated to Nagoya City in December 2016. She moved there with some enthusiasm but not for the city. It was not until half a year after that she started seeing Nagoya for its own beauty.

Leira Matubis

HOW TO USE THIS BOOK

The Greater Than a Tourist book series was written by someone who has lived in an area for over three months. The goal of this book is to help travelers either dream or experience different locations by providing opinions from a local. The author has made suggestions based on their own experiences. Please do your own research before traveling to the area in case the suggested places are unavailable.

Leira Matubis

\>TOURIST

FROM THE PUBLISHER

Traveling can be one of the most important parts of a person's life. The anticipation and memories that you have are some of the best. As a publisher of the Greater Than a Tourist book series, as well as the popular 50 Things to Know book series, we strive to help you learn about new places, spark your imagination, and inspire you. Wherever you are and whatever you do I wish you safe, fun, and inspiring travel.

Lisa Rusczyk Ed. D.
CZYK Publishing

Leira Matubis

>TOURIST

OUR STORY

Traveling is a passion of the "Greater than a Tourist" series creator. Lisa studied abroad in college, and for their honeymoon Lisa and her husband toured Europe. During her travels to Malta, an older man tried to give her some advice based on his own experience living on the island since he was a young boy. She was not sure if she should talk to the stranger but was interested in his advice. When traveling to some places she was wary to talk to locals because she was afraid that they weren't being genuine. Through her travels, Lisa learned how much locals had to share with tourists. Lisa created the "Greater Than a Tourist" book series to help connect people with locals. A topic that locals are very passionate about sharing.

Leira Matubis

>TOURIST

WELCOME TO
> TOURIST

Leira Matubis

>TOURIST

INTRODUCTION

Traveling is not for the eyes,
it's for the mind and the heart.

In the summer of 2017, a friend of mine came to Japan for a week-long trip. To my surprise, he decided to stay in Nagoya for the first half. That odd choice of destination stirred up some intriguing thoughts. First of all, I couldn't comprehend the reason Tokyo, Osaka, and a multitude of other more well known places were overlooked. It also meant that I, duty-bound by friendship, would have to show him around.

Nagoya is usually the 4th or 5th choice for tourists visiting Japan. It's the fourth biggest city where big groups of tourists are not a common sight. With only 3 tourist information centers, one can't help but think it's deliberately kept that way. Frankly speaking, I myself had a difficult time thinking of what to do and where to take my friend. Imagine what I had to do to write this book.

So I mustered some courage. A few days after my friend informed me about his trip, I asked him via

Leira Matubis

Messenger. I remember watching the dots blink while going through possible responses in my head. I shook at the many unlikely reasons and then it occurred to me that the most obvious reason was to spend time with some old friends. How touching. Finally, the eagerly awaited ding arrived and his terse reply read "Cheap flights."

>TOURIST

1. ENTER THROUGH NAGOYA

Just like my friend over here, if you're looking to visit Japan, want to maximize your budget, and worried about the potentially massive expenses, why don't you try Nagoya? It's a safe bet. Flights are moderately cheaper and the location is a gateway to neighboring and distant locations. Major train lines and bus routes connect the city and make other prefectures easily accessible.

Whenever I travel around Japan, the first thing I check is highway bus routes and fares. The Shinkansen is a marvel and it is undeniably the fastest and most convenient way to get around. It's a great experience, however it's also the most expensive. Flights to far-flung destinations are even cheaper than the Shinkansen. My personal preference, taking the bus, is a more economical alternative.

On my 24th birthday, I took the Willer Bus to Osaka. It was fall and as a treat to myself, I went to see the changing foliage. The bus ride was such an inexpensively delightful way to start and end the trip. The reclinable seats were a cut above the rest. They came equipped with a canopy, a small pillow, charging ports, a foot rest and leg room that my over 6-foot brother-in-law will likely appreciate. The distance was almost 200 kilometers but the journey was gentle and unhurried, passing through mountains covered with sheets of green and red atop a cloudless slate backdrop.

Due to its central location, numerous interesting places can be visited from Nagoya. In its immediate vicinity are Gifu Prefecture, well-known for the historic villages in UNESCO World Heritage Site Shirakawa-go; Mie Prefecture, which houses Japan's most sacred shrine Ise Jingu; and Shizuoka Prefecture, famed for Japan's highest peak Mount Fuji.

2. STAY IN NAGOYA

A few months after moving, Nagoya seemed like a wet blanket. Having already visited popular spots and done all the cool activities suggested by travel sites in such a short time, there was nothing and nowhere left for me to go so I started looking for buses to Tokyo for a one-week trip. There was a distant thought of possibly relocating but that was many a ways off.

In my line of work, teaching students from different cities is a daily occurrence. Because Nagoya is a hub of manufacturing and shipping companies, many employees from Tokyo are sent to live and work here. I wanted to hear their thoughts so I asked the pressing question, "Which do you prefer?"

Most of them had the same response: Nagoya. When asked why, they would reason out that Nagoya has a good balance of urban and rural areas, that it was smaller, that it was not crowded, and other typical reasons. The most concerning one was that the cost of living is unreasonably steep in Tokyo. But undeterred, I pressed on and experienced it for myself.

My trip resulted in the realization that my students were right all along. No doubt, Tokyo is a fascinating city. There are more fun things and more interesting places in Tokyo. More glitz, more glamour, more flare and infinitely more than any other place I've visited but by the end of my trip, I was dying to go back.

There are many things Nagoya doesn't have. There isn't a Disneyland, a Shibuya crossing, wildly themed restaurants or as many English-speakers. Nor does it have that palpable urban sprawl, big city energy but rather it's a small and cozy city that has a gentle and welcoming atmosphere that makes me feel that it is as much mine as my own house.

Leira Matubis

3. AVOID AUGUST

My second time in Nagoya was in 2016. I had not seen my boyfriend in over a year so I bought a ticket, very impulsively I should say. On previous trips, we would decide together and keep each other fully informed of dates, flight times and any diversions from the plan. But on that occasion, I decided to be spontaneous. No plans, no discussion, no due diligence. I clicked on the "PAY" button and my fate was sealed.

On the day of my flight, I took one final look at my phone before take-off. It was a late morning in August, the wettest month of the year. My old but still trusty Blackberry said it was 26 degrees Celsius outside. There had been erratic rainfall all week which had brought with it a cool breeze. It would have been a lovely cool day except for the drizzle.

Nagoya was in the peak of summer. And like majority of people from tropical countries, I loved it. Pleasant sunshine, crisp dry air and picture-perfect silhouettes were what I looked forward to. The heat grows on you, live with it too long and you learn to love it.

Four hours later, I arrived in Nagoya with great expectations only to be greeted with a damp forehead, moist underarms, sweaty palms and a desperate need to change my shirt. The temperature was a scorching 34 degrees Celsius and humidity at 80%. Ironically, that day was hotter than the average temperature in Manila. Up until then, I had loved the summer.

With temperatures playing above 30 degrees Celsius in daytime, my limited gallivanting was done mostly at night. I would go out in the late afternoon and take the last train home. On some nights when the sun wasn't so ruthless, I would take my boyfriend's bike for a long overdue spin. Nonetheless, I thought the places were sights to behold and for some, even better.

4. KAKIGORI

Like I said, August is a time you want to avoid but know that it's only because of the harsh heat and relentless humidity. If you do find yourself here, don't lock yourself indoors. It isn't as dreadful as you may think. Put on sunscreen, grab a fan and a parasol because there are a number of interesting experiences that only this hot season can offer.

First and foremost is kakigori. This is a Japanese summer treat similar to the Filipino halo-halo and the Korean bingsu. A feathery hill of ice shavings with drizzles of velvety syrup is a sure-fire way to beat the intense heat. A red brush-stroked character resembling an asterisk on a field of white and blue is a sign that stores are offering kakigori.

Arguably the best kakigori in Nagoya is from Fruits Boutique Goto near Ikeshita station on the Higashiyama Line. Primarily a fruit shop, it offers a wide selection of fruit flavors and fresh toppings. Because their frozen creations are a delight to the eyes and taste buds, this place is constantly flocked by clammy locals hoping to stay cool.

Another place that serves equally scrumptious kakigori is Kakigori Senmonten Andoryu. Expertly hidden in the Osu Shopping district, Andoryu is a small unsophisticated shop that serves tasty melts-in-your-mouth shaved ice. Much like the adjoining shopping district where it's easy to get lost, the shop makes for a great treasure hunt.

>TOURIST

5. THE GRAND SUMO TOURNAMENT

In the early summer days of June, random sumo wrestlers start popping up. Clad in colorful kimonos, they can be seen taking the train or walking leisurely in and around the city. The wrestlers are very easy to spot, distinguishable by gigantic portly figures and sleek black hair in a topknot. The emergence of these wrestlers is a sign that sumo season has arrived in Nagoya.

Sumo, in its early years, was a sacred rite in Shinto shrines where humans were said to be wrestling with pagan spirits. It became a form of entertainment centuries after but since modern Japan, it has evolved into a professional sport practiced all around the country. With roots tracing as far back as the 16th century, the sport maintains ceremonial rituals derived from ancient Shinto worship like salt purification.

Every year in July, the Aichi Prefectural Gymnasium, outside of the Nagoya Castle grounds, hosts the Grand Sumo tournaments in a span of 15 days as part of the six sequential tournaments in Japan. The others being in Tokyo in January, May and September; Osaka in March; and Fukuoka in November.

The Grand Sumo tournaments are an elusive deal so it's best to buy tickets ahead of time. There is no reason to wait as seats sell out quickly especially weekend and final matches. Japanese cushioned floor seats, although literally a pain in the butt, are also more favorable than chairs as they are closer to the ring. The sumo matches are a full-day event but many enthusiasts arrive late, after the lower division matches have finished. Remember to charge your phone or bring some books as the ceremonial rites between matches can be a bit drawn-out.

6. FIREWORKS FESTIVALS

Hanami is to spring, as hanabi is to summer. Just like how popular cherry blossom viewing is in April, not a weekend will go by without a fireworks show somewhere in Japan in August. Formerly used as a tool to keep evil spirits at bay, fireworks have since become an essential part of the Japanese summer festivities with some attracting hundreds of thousands of onlookers.

Hanabi matsuris or fireworks festivals are places where families and friends can be carefree. Many

>TOURIST

couples also find these festivals an ideal option for dates. Women and young girls, all dolled up and parading their colorful yukatas, stand out from the rest of the crowd. Stalls of festival food like takoyaki line the streets and goldfish scooping booths are flocked by eager children.

Possibly the biggest hanabi matsuri in Nagoya is the Nagoya Minato Matsuri, held at Nagoya Garden Pier. The grand celebrations started in the 1950's to uplift the people's spirits following the devastating destruction from World War II. Although small when compared to other matsuris around the country, this humble festival still attracts a whopping audience of 370,000 people on average. Spectators gather on the docks to watch the extravagant display of some 3000 fireworks.

As you would expect from any major event, there are some drawbacks to attending these wildly popular festivals. The Japanese can be very competitive when it comes to viewing spots. Many will arrive hours before just to put a blanket down on the grass areas. Public transportation and parking spaces are also causes for concern. Luckily, my boyfriend's office is right next to the pier so we never have to fight for a parking space.

7. HIGASHI BETSUIN TEMPLE

On one of my late afternoon bike rides, I was on my way to Osu-Kannon for a shopping spree. Following a 10-minute uphill sprint, I slowed down on the sidewalk of a bustling intersection. My breathing had gotten heavy and there were many cars whizzing past so I dragged the bike to a nearby temple to catch my breath. I glanced inside the wide-open gates from where I was panting. There were grey-haired women in pastel-colored kimonos dancing and singing on an elevated stage with a group of younger men beating drums in the back. Of course, the curious me parked my bike beside hundreds of others and went inside.

The stage was set in the middle of the large fine-gravel grounds. Surrounding it were ordinary people and children following the intricate hand and arm movements of the dancers. To its right were entertaining games for children and a few stalls selling handicrafts, trinkets and fans. To its left were compact stalls selling refreshments, assortments of bread, kakigori and takoyaki. The takoyaki looked irresistible so I bought a plate and wandered off.

The stately Higashi Betsuin Temple was across from the stage. There was a broad set of stairs leading inside where a few monks in black robes stood to watch the festivities. There were more footpaths on either side of the temple but I ate my takoyaki, only wondering where they led.

The dances and the drums continued, every minute more people joined. I tried my hand in a few games and bought some bread to take home. When I left I could still hear the faint sound of beating drums over screeching tires. How long I stayed I don't exactly remember but I never got to shop at Osu-kannon like I planned.

8. SUBWAYS & RAILS

Anyone who has traveled to a metropolitan city has been lost at least once using the subway. On my trip to Tokyo however, I was lost for a face-palmable amount. I'm no navigator nor do I have a strong reliable sense of direction but Nagoya had always been uncomplicated. Getting the hang of the subway map is quite easy because it was designed using the 8-color Crayola box.

I'm not implying that it's impossible to get lost but taking the wrong train usually only happens above ground on the Meitetsu, JR or other lines that extend from the city center all the way to the suburbs,

Leira Matubis

neighboring cities or prefectures. Using these lines is inevitable as many tourist spots are along them so to avoid mishaps, be attentive to the train announcements, routes, platform numbers and express trains.

One exception is the Aonami Line which is effortless. It always arrives on time, has only one route and has clear English announcements. Aonami is a relatively new line that started operating passenger trains in the early 2000's. It stretches from Nagoya Station, servicing the quiet suburbs where I live, and terminates near Nagoya Port. The whole ride lasts for 24 minutes without any connections to other lines. Surely many of you will take it going to Legoland which is, please note, the last stop.

However for accommodations, you might want to stay within short walking distance of major stations that give access to different lines. It goes without saying that Nagoya and Kanayama are the biggest but there's also Sakae on a rail and 2 subway lines; Chikusa on a subway and a rail line and Ozone with a whopping 4 connections to a subway line, 2 rails and the rail/sky-bus line.

>TOURIST

9. THE RAIL / SKYBUS

Hard to put an image to the words, I know. I couldn't wrap my head around it the first time too so try and visualize this. You're sitting on a cold metal bench in a barely occupied elevated station waiting for your connection. Suddenly, you notice blinding headlights coming your way so you avert your attention to the only other people in the station. The breaks screech to a full stop, the doors clank open and you get up as your eyes open to a city bus docked in front of you. What? A bus?

Yes, a bus. The puzzling Yutorito Line is the only guided bus line in Japan. It's complete with wickets, platforms, an elevated guideway and it's even part of the subway map. Officially known as Guideway Shimada Bus Line, which would have spared many tourists the confusion, it runs four different routes from Ozone station, initially through the dedicated viaduct and later joining other buses on the street.

A good excuse to use this line is the Togokusan Fruit Park which is on the Yutorito route. The bus ride on its own is amusing. Because the guideway is elevated and the immediate surroundings are that of a bus, it feels like public transportation years into the future.

Leira Matubis

10. FRUIT PICKING AT TOGOKUSAN

Although the entire park is laden with cherry trees which makes it a spring favorite, the Togokusan Fruit Park is actually a multi-purpose agricultural park that can be visited anytime of the year. Based at the foot of the highest peak in Nagoya, Togoku Mountain, it accommodates diverse species of fruits, plants, trees and flowers.

The entire park, in spring, is instagrammable. Shutter clicks can be heard anywhere from the orchards all the way to the fishing corner on the far end. There are two large large interconnected domes that greet you once you cross the north gates. Aptly titled 'Orchard of the World', it houses tropical fruit trees not commonly found in Japan such as jackfruit, dragon fruit, passion fruit and mango. Outdoors, they offer visitors the experience to pick organically grown familiar fruits like plum, apple, persimmon and kiwi during harvest season. Loads of blooming flowers are always on display to amaze visitors without fail.

Apart from that, the park also has a spacious field for regularly organized fairs to exhibit fruit art, sell local

>TOURIST

produce and hold workshops. The rolling grassy area is for groups to have picnics while the restaurants behind the domes are for sampling an array of freshly picked fruits.

11. TOKUGAWA ART MUSEUM

A private museum located near Ozone Station and established in 1935, the Tokugawa Art Museum is now the 4th oldest privately-endowed museum in Japan. The museum turned 80 years old in 2015 with their current galleries and facilities completed in the 1897 restoration to commemorate their 50th anniversary.

The proud Tokugawa Art Museum reflects the very pride of the Tokugawa family, from which the extensive collection of over 12,000 items were gathered. Ancient heirlooms, furnishings, art and other objects characterize this historic and well-documented collection. One exhibit houses armor, swords, helmets, decorations and cannons used by the vassals and lords of the first shogun, Tokugawa Ieyasu. Another room is a faithful replica of a Japanese lord's ceremonial room. Traditionally used to receive guests and host banquets, the windowed room is complete with tatami or woven straw floors, sliding painted wall panels and a raised seating section for the master of the house. The museum looks like a set for a movie set in feudal Japan.

In another section of the museum, the Hosa library holds a vast library of written materials from the Edo period, including Tokugawa Ieyasu's personal collection of 3000 volumes of Japanese, Chinese and Dutch books. Outdoors, there is a magnificent traditional garden with a small waterfall and stone paths. Very much like what a Japanese lord would have outside of his residence, the garden is a great place to view vibrant flowers during blooming season.

12. NAGOYA CASTLE

Nagoya Jo, or Nagoya Castle in English, was first built in the outset of Edo period. Rebuilt in 1600's, this castle characterized the pride and power of the most important branch of the Tokugawa family. The castle town around it eventually expanded and transformed into the fourth largest city in Japan. Now, it is the biggest and most historical attraction of Nagoya City.

Used as a strategic location for defensive military tactics, the castle has seen its fair share of war but in 1945 during World War II, the US Air Forces brought forth the biggest destruction it has ever endured.

>TOURIST

Because the main castle and towers were nearly burned down, the people of Nagoya requested that the proud symbol be reconstructed. The beloved castle's concrete structure now goes back only 50 years ago and houses surviving photographs, screen paintings and maps.

Many hidden features can be found all over the grounds of the palace. A tea house is placed in the middle of a beautiful garden in the grounds, where you can participate in an authentic tea ceremony. Mini museums are scattered around, exhibiting different kinds of historical and cultural items. These museums are a great stop especially during summer because, apart from being air-conditioned, there are nearby vending machines and outdoor seating.

13. STONE WALLS

You may be wondering what those odd carvings are on the stones that support the castle. It's hard not to notice because they are everywhere from the main gate, all the way to the main keep. Many lords under the domain of the Tokugawa family were ordered to help build the castle and as a sort of signature, these proud lords carved their stones to distinguish their contribution from others.

On the fourth floor of the main keep, a realistic representation of how these lords and their vassals constructed the impressive stone reinforcements are in the form of an interactive model. A huge rectangular stone is tied with a rope and pulled by three strong men who require a hand from visitors. The rope extends to the other side where a platform stands for anyone who wants to test their strength. Complete with a timer and a digital meter, you can find out if you would have been a worthy Japanese laborer in the Edo period.

14. THE KINSHACHI

When you enter the main keep, the first thing you will see is a huge statue of a golden dolphin. Upstairs, the floors are filled with more shining golden dolphins varying in sizes. Even the roofs of the castle are adorned with these cute creatures. You will have seen it wearing station officer uniform somewhere in the subway, reminding passengers of public transportation etiquette, or on a souvenir box in a kiosk in Nagoya Station.

The Kinshachi are legendary creatures able to summon water at will and kill fire at a flick of a finger, or fin. Any Japanese can easily identify these adorable

> TOURIST

creatures as Nagoya's icon. On the fourth floor of Nagoya Castle, a playful kinshachi lets visitors ride and take photos with it. The top floor is an observatory where you can see neighboring areas and spy on locals through the coin-operated binoculars. Many kinshachi can also be seen around here in the forms of figurines, keychains, socks, fridge magnets, fans and chopsticks.

15. 400-YEAR OLD SAMURAI

Please don't take it literally like my sister did. They aren't actually 400 years old, they are actors portraying the famous names from the Sengoku or the Warring States period of Japan. The Great Unifiers and other Samurai Kings are brought back to life in the grounds of Nagoya Castle everyday.

These Samurai Kings nonchalantly wander the castle in distinct traditional garb, occasionally displaying their prowess in combat. Most days, they can be seen fending off intruders, stalking rival ninjas or merely settling disputes through intense performances. Be warned, they will not hesitate to unsheathe their swords if they sense any threat to the castle... or its cleanliness.

On idle days when these Samurai Kings aren't occupied by strategic planning, they help keep the castle grounds spick and span. Picking up trash, raking leaves and reminding stationed stalls and visitors to keep it clean. To boot, they are a jolly group that is fond of taking pictures with and directing lost visitors. Every now and then, they will indulge inquisitive guests with recounts of their tales and adventures that led to modern Japan.

16. THE NAMELESS THEATRE

Talking about actors, there is another diverse group of people from different parts of the world who enjoy pretending to be others. The group has appeared as big names from Shakespearean classics like Romeo and Juliet, A Midsummer Night's Dream and Much Ado about Nothing.

Luckily last year, I had the pleasure of watching their production of Shakespeare's Othello. Held in a dimly-lit modest theatre in Chikusa, the stage was encircled by a slope of seats. It was bare and the costumes were contemporary but the lights were spectacular. As if they had a mind of their own, they transformed the stage into a sea of blood, clouds and fire as the play transitioned from scene to scene. The cast's modern and meticulous take of destructive jealousy and manipulation in Othello complemented the minimalist vibe of the play.

Bold risks are taken and pulled off admirably by this interesting mix of foreign and Japanese creative minds. The Nameless Theatre has ironically and successfully made its presence known in Nagoya's art scene.

17. KABUKI CAFE

Okay, more about acting. While Shakespeare was busy being a playwright in the 16th century thousands of miles away, a new form of entertainment was beginning to gain popularity in Japan. Characterized by stylized drama and elaborate make-up, the Kabuki was developed to entertain the then largely insular Japanese nation.

The history of Kabuki dates way back to 1600, when the first Kabuki shows centered on indecent humor and were performed by prostitutes. The upper echelon samurai didn't approve of the suggestive themes and didn't appreciate its ability to set trends among the major population so eventually female performers were replaced with all-male casts. In many ways, the outlandish style of Kabuki is believed to have brought forth the similarly eccentric fashion culture of Harajuku.

    Nagoya Za, a cozy cafe ten minutes away from Nagoya Station, brings back the authentic animated Kabuki performances from the Edo period. Except for the frequent brawls and name calling, the shows perfectly capture the undisciplined impression of Kabuki. The hour-long performances are all in their native tongue but the wacky performers act with such exaggeration that barely any Japanese is needed to enjoy the show. At the end, the cast sits down to have an informative chat about Kabuki history, enact crazy improvised skits or just to get to know the audience. The show is rich with humor, daring stunts and falling prop debris it's impossible not to crack up.

18. OSU SHOPPING

    One of the best places to shop in Nagoya is the Osu Shopping Street. Whether you're buying souvenirs or simply shopping for yourself, here is where everything is in one huge shopping district. It isn't exactly just one street as the name implies, but rather, it's a series of intersecting alleys and streets stretching from Kamimaezu Station to Osu Kannon Station.

>TOURIST

All kinds of different shops for different interests can be found in Osu, the center of entertainment, street fashion and pop culture here in Nagoya. Having been around for 400 years as a commercial area, it now boasts over 1,200 establishments from huge appliance shops, affordable clothing brands, entertainment complexes, and specialty cafes. Various events are regularly held in Osu, the biggest being the summer festival in August and the most frequent being the antique market held every 18th and 28th of the month.

The growing youth and pop culture has also largely influenced many shops in Osu. Now catering to a huge number of anime, manga, and video game fans, many cosplayers can sometimes be seen parading in the streets. Maid cafes and other specialty shops have also been popping around the area. Because of the popular trend of Jpop girl groups, the 20-member Osu Super Idol Unit has been an active presence in the district since its first appearance in 2010.

19. FEED THE PIGEONS

Many pigeons think of Nagoya as their home. Many roam the streets, parks and residential areas, scavenging dumpsters and garbage bags for food. Some antagonize bento-carrying passengers in the platforms of major stations. Periodically, few get lost on train tracks or build nests on utility poles causing serious delays. There are so many that it's considered a dilemma.

But many temples and shrines around the city are safe havens for pigeons. They congregate at greenery-filled environments where they are welcomed warmly by monks and treated kindly by visitors. Like the famed Osu-Kannon Temple, pigeons find these sacred sites a refuge from their biped foes.

It's hard to imagine Osu-Kannon without the pigeons. The red and white intersecting beams and curved pagodas of the temple are favorite spots to perch on. For animal lovers, feeding and chasing them around is unforgettable. These friendly creatures are already accustomed to human interaction, many will stay on the ground even when running after them. Some won't take flight unless you slide open the shelf to grab some bird feed, in which case they come flying right to you. For a handful of birdseed at 50 yen, they can get the royal treatment from tourists.

>TOURIST

20. ISE SHRINE

The biggest and most sacred place of worship in Japan is Ise Jingu or Ise Grand Shrine. Located in the neighboring Mie Prefecture, Ise Jingu is a massive complex of over 125 shrines in Ise City. The easily accessible outer shrines are 10 minutes away from Ise-shi Station, compared to the inner shrines which take about an hour or two of walking in a moderate pace.

According to the second oldest book in Japan, 2000 years ago, the daughter of the emperor set out to look for the best site to worship the sun goddess, Amaterasu. After twenty years of searching, she settled on Ise City, after Amaterasu herself whispered to her and chose the secluded land near the mountains and the sea. Today, the inner sanctuary of Ise Grand Shrine is the permanent home for Amaterasu, closed off by multiple sets of fences; and the sacred mirror, one of the Imperial Regalia, gifts from the sun goddess to the first emperor of Japan.

Upon passing the Uji Bridge, a 100-meter long wooden bridge, the serene forests surrounding the path provide for an extremely religious air. Visitors participate in purification rites by washing their hands in the blessed water of Isuzugawa River.

Leira Matubis

An interesting factoid about the Ise Grand Shrine is that it is rebuilt every twenty years. It is believed that rebuilding makes the shrines eternal, all the while preserving the original architecture and passing down traditional carpentry skills to the following generation. This means that the new shrines are built exactly as it was, without a single piece of metal, only interlocking beams and pegs. The practice of rebuilding the Ise Grand Shrine has been done since a thousand years ago and realizes the important Shinto belief of death and rebirth.

21. ATSUTA SHRINE

Second in size to Ise Jingu, Atsuta Jingu is where another one of the Imperial regalias, the sword Kusanagi-no-tsurugi, is enshrined. Visited annually by 9 million people, this list would not be complete without this historical shrine.

First built around 1900 years ago, Atsuta Jingu is believed to be a protector of agriculture. Located in the lush farm lands of western Aichi, many festivals held here are closely related to farming and agriculture. Grand planting ceremonies are an essential part of these festivals.

>TOURIST

One of its biggest festivals is Rei-Sai Festival on the 5th of June. Exhibitions of judo, archery and fencing are presented to express thanks to the gods. Traditional dances are also performed with music from Japanese flutes and drums. Particularly interesting are the huge lantern floats displayed at the entrances of the shrine.

Atsuta Jingu was bombed in World War II and afterwards rebuilt in the 1950's but not everything from the grounds was destroyed. A 1,300 year old camphor tree sits inside the grounds, believed to have been planted by a renowned Buddhist priest. There are also exhibits inside the shrine that house ancient relics, sacred garments and important documents from historical Japan. The grounds are vast with streams flowing through, a very spiritual place good for a stroll and a lesson on history.

22. SHIROTORI GARDEN

A beautiful traditional Japanese garden is a 10-minute walk away from Atsuta Jingu. The Shirotori Garden imitates the scenic landscapes of central Japan and puts them all together in less than 4 hectares. The garden gives visitors a look at how Japan was in former times.

Leira Matubis

Throughout the year, the Shirotori Garden transforms into splendid views along with the seasons. In fall, people visit the garden to see the red and gold leaves. Cherry blossoms are another popular sight. In the winter, the gorgeous rock arrangements and gardens are covered in a sheet of soft snow.

The ponds are home to charming colored carp that you can interact with. If there are fish, of course there is fish feed. Watch the fish go crazy and flock towards you once those grains hit the water. Ducks and turtles occasionally show up to compete with the fish.

The name 'shirotori' when translated means 'white swan' which is the inspiration behind the graceful tea rooms in the center of the garden. These rooms regularly hold traditional tea ceremonies where visitors can taste authentic green tea along with other Japanese sweets.

23. VISIT AT NIGHT

One such place that is better to visit when the sun has gone down is Sakae. This place is widely considered as the beating heart of the city. Its streets are lined with high-end luxury brands, lavish department stores and flashing lights that tempt you to spend,

spend, spend. Here is where many locals hang out on Fridays and Saturdays for a night of gutsy fun and all-out partying.

Prior to working in Japan, I had never visited Sakae in the daytime. Basking in its illustrious charm was my ideal night out. Under streaks of dim colored lights and shadows, I would stroll the streets and watch as hundreds of people walk into stores empty-handed and come out lugging shopping bags. There is a mysterious force that envelops everyone in its proximity. On many occasions, I too, could not escape its grasp. Passing by a store one gloomy evening, black coat perched perfectly on a headless mannequin caught my attention. The spotlight in the display window focused on another significantly more expensive coat beside it. After much deliberation, I went home tens of thousands of yen poorer but at least I got two fancy new coats.

But now, Sakae is my home 5 days a week. On the other side of Sakae are white-collar offices and tall buildings like the NHK Tower and Meiji Yasuda Seimei Nagoya. Seas of well-dressed men and women crowd the subways and streets in the early mornings. I still feel its force in the daytime, not as daunting so I've learned to control myself. Where I used to indulge in excessive spending is now just a view from a dusty floor-length window in my office building.

24. THE NEST

As a foreigner with pitiful Japanese ability, I rarely get to interact with locals in their own language in a social environment. Most of the day, as best I can I avoid speaking Japanese altogether but so far I've very creatively managed my day-to-day life with the limited phrases I know. Every once in a while when I get an unexpected urge to exercise my Japanese, Elephant's Nest is my pub of choice.

Located near Fushimi Station in Sakae, this old-fashioned British pub draws an equal balance of foreign and Japanese customers. Adorned with UK flags, glass windows stained with coats-of-arms and a well-stocked bar, they offer scores of beers on tap such as Kirin, Guinness and Kilkenny. Dartboards hang on one side of the pub and big flat screens tuned in on the latest soccer game, free for any customer to use. Each month, they revitalize their cocktail lineup, it's not at all strange to see a dead snake in a bottle.

On Sunday nights, they host language exchange parties where people from all over the world gather to

>TOURIST

drink, socialize and hone their language skills. I attend them whenever I feel in the mood for an engaging conversation. So far, I've met some really cool people here, a craftsman who makes charming handmade leather products, a magician who can make coins disappear, an underground scene rapper and his producer, and perhaps the most interesting of all, an unmarried middle-aged man who has nearly traveled the world, can speak 8 different languages and loves to salsa.

25. THE ROCK

Just last year, an Australian coworker and friend decided to go back home to possibly study again after some time of working in Nagoya. Before he left, the other teachers and I got together, unsurprisingly, in an Australian bar behind Chunichi Building in Sakae. It was my first time in The Rock, befittingly named after Uluru or Ayers Rock in Australia.

I have never been to Australia, nor had I ever tasted any of their food. According to my Aussie friend, the bar had an authentic and excellent menu. As per his suggestion, we ordered their best sellers and they were all superb. The Meat Pie was moist and flavorful, the

Chicken Parmy's original tomato sauce was delectable and the Aussie Nachos overflowed with toppings.

After a few cans of Victoria Bitters, we got some of their more exotic choices, the Crocodile and Kangaroo Mini Burgers. At first, I was hesitant to try their beloved animals but heck, it was great. The kangaroo meat had a strong flavor and a chewy texture while the crocodile meat was very much like rubbery chicken but with a mild taste of fish. Nonetheless, both were well seasoned and complemented the coleslaw and house-baked buns nicely.

If you're looking to interact with locals in English, The Rock is the perfect place. Multiculturally staffed, this Aussie bar is an expat favorite. They regularly have live broadcasts of rugby, soccer, baseball matches and more. On Sundays, they transform into a live house to showcase the impressive talent of local musicians.

26. SHOOTERS

Another great place to have fun conversations is Shooters, an American sports bar that serves possibly the best western food in Nagoya. It has a very friendly and relaxed atmosphere serviced by a kind multicultural staff. This bar has been around since 1996 and is now

>TOURIST

the longest running and most successful international bar in Nagoya.

Primarily a sports bar, Shooters is where sports enthusiasts congregate for the latest matches. Their long standing tradition of opening the bar outside business hours to broadcast the NFL Super Bowl live is truly remarkable. In these early winter mornings of February, football fans enjoy a full breakfast buffet, a generous drink bar all while watching the most eagerly awaited program in the history of American television.

On ordinary days, Shooters also lets their customers try out their hand in a few indoor sports. There are electronic dart boards and billiard tables on one side of the bar. Talented artists are frequently invited to showcase their music on weekend nights. The customers are mostly friendly foreigners always ready for a chat but they also attract a fair number of Japanese customers.

At Shooters, ordering is always a difficult task because there are so many drinks and dishes to choose from. With a menu of over 10 pages, there's always something new to try every time you visit. For first time visitors, the Pulled-Pork Sliders and Baby Back Ribs tastes as good as it looks on the menu. The Tex-Mex range is also popular but if you can't decide, order 4-

way Sampler Plate for a taste of everything. Don't forget to get a side of their beans too, it's the best!

27. NAGOYA CITY SCIENCE MUSEUM

Less than 10 minutes from Fushimi Station on the Higashiyama Line is an odd looking metal ball that is the Nagoya City Science Museum. Children just love this place because science is made fun and interactive but it's also for adults to enjoy. The entire museum is filled with dials, knobs, buttons, handles for visitors to learn something about physics, electronics, anatomy, you name it, this museum has it.

The highlight of the Nagoya City Science museum is that huge metal ball. The second largest planetarium in the world, just 7 feet shy of the first, is 115 feet in diameter and can accommodate 350 people. The planetarium uses live narrations and full-dome projections discussing varying topics like astronomy, space travel and seasonal stars. Apart from being the second largest, it uses the most sophisticated and the highest quality equipment to replicate the starry night sky.

>TOURIST

Narrated completely in Japanese, the one-hour long programs are hard to enjoy for foreigners, frankly even to some Japanese. A huge portion of the audience can be heard snoring partly because of the extremely comfortable and wide seats that recline to almost 180 degrees and rotate more than 180 degrees, giving the audience the whole range of napping positions.

Apart from the planetarium, the Nagoya City Science Museum also has exhibits that pop-up depending on the time of the year. When I visited last winter, my boyfriend and I, together with 20 other people, were locked in a room with a temperature of 30 degrees below zero for 10 minutes. In the basement of the museum, we watched our hysterical doodles come to life in a large lit screen in a dark room.

28. HIGASHIYAMA ZOO

Also located on the Higashiyama Line is a huge commercial facility including a zoo, botanical gardens, an amusement park, its own monorail and a tower. The Higashiyama Zoo was first opened in 1937 and was instantaneously a big success. The 60-hectare facility holds many records to date. It's the second busiest zoo in Japan after Tokyo's Ueno Zoo, one of Asia's biggest

Leira Matubis

zoos, home to Shabani, the world's most handsome gorilla, and the first zoo to introduce koalas to Japan.

The massive zoo is home to over 500 different species including reptiles, mammals, fish, birds and insects. A few of the most visited are the MacKenzie Valley wolf and the rare Persian leopard but probably the best attraction is a male western lowland gorilla.

Shabani was born in the Netherlands and raised in Australia before relocating to Nagoya in 2007, when he was known for balancing and walking on tightropes. However in 2015, he gained a different image thanks to photogenic pictures of him circulating on the internet. His brooding eyes and odd charm led to a sudden boost in the park's female visitors. Many common Japanese slang for handsome male humans have been used to label Shabani since then, by far the most used is ikemen or roughly 'hunk'.

Shabani can usually be seen lounging around, charming female visitors or playing with two children, Annie and Kiyomasu. On other days, he's be busy promoting his product line of cakes and candies, attending photoshoots for print ad or just being the spokesperson of Higashiyama Zoo. He's a modest and friendly guy, who enjoys his internet fame, even after having been compared to George Clooney.

>TOURIST

Despite being well-maintained and filled with exciting things, the park is continually redeveloped to provide residents with more comfortable accommodations and to give visitors a more exciting experience. Adjacent to the Zoo lies a botanical garden with Japan's oldest glasshouse. In the large garden, fields of cherry blossoms, camellias, and wildflowers are cultivated. The gardens are designed in the traditional Japanese landscape with ponds and plants make for very powerful views.

Another attraction is the Higashiyama Tower set atop Mount Higashi and provides a superview of the zoo, the gardens and the surrounding areas. At the ground floor, you can indulge in a huge selection of popular Japanese and special sweets. Up at the top of the tower, visitors can enjoy Italian and French dining all while viewing the warm colors of the setting sun.

29. TOYOTA COMMEMORATIVE MUSEUM

Did you know that the world renowned automobile brand Toyota started out as a textile company? The red-bricked building of the Toyota Commemorative Museum, also on the Higashiyama Line, was originally

Leira Matubis

a factory that manufactured a broad range of textile machineries. The history of Toyota isn't widely known so this place teaches you some really surprising facts about this Japanese brand.

The Toyota Commemorative Museum has two main areas. First, the Textile Machinery Pavilion, which houses around 90 machines and displays the incredible precision and accuracy of the machines. Various techniques used over the years are shown like three-dimensional cloth weaving, cotton-spinning and the circular loom which was developed by the company in 1906.

On the other area is the Automobile Pavilion dedicated to showing how production of automobiles still use the same mechanics as the power looms. It also compares how the production of car components have changed and have been influenced by the use of advanced technologies. There is a number of cars on display showing the transition of automobiles from the first generation to the new hybrid models.

Another interesting part of the museum is the violin-playing robot which was first presented in Shanghai World Expo as part of Toyota's future projects. The company develops a number of different robots to support and add convenience to human lives in the spirit of research and creativity.

30. NORITAKE GARDEN

In 1876, a trading company exported handcrafted Japanese antiques and discovered that particularly popular in the USA were decorated ceramics from Seto City in Aichi. Eventually the company focused on producing more of the fancy western style tableware and thus, the world famous ceramics brand, Noritake, was born.

With over 100 years of producing high-quality and exquisite plates, cups, bowls and saucers, Noritake has perfected the art of ceramics. The signature product of this world-renowned brand is hand painted dinnerware. Formerly factory grounds some 15 minutes from Nagoya Station, the Noritake Garden is now a museum with a large display of vases and plates from the Meiji Era when the company began and European style tableware from the Taisho and Showa Eras when the company was making a name for itself.

The vast grounds of Noritake Garden boast a craft center where visitors can see up close how bone chinas are intricately decorated. Visitors are also free to join workshops where chances to design ceramics are given to participants. In another part, handcrafted products are closely compared to mass manufactured versions. The delicacy of handcrafting is also contrasted to advanced technologies with the results relatively distinct.

Outside of the craft center, there is a French and Italian restaurant serving gourmet food on Noritake tableware. An outlet also offers a wide selection at bargain prices. The landscape surrounding the red-bricked facilities have become the distinguishing feature of the garden.

31. TASTE FRESH BEER

Without a shadow of a doubt, the Japanese people love to drink. Alcohol is something they drink on a daily basis. There are even vending machines in my neighborhood dedicated to selling alcoholic drinks. There are vending machines for cigarettes too. You'd be surprised what else they sell on vending machines.

While we were some 1500 miles apart, I was genuinely concerned about my boyfriend's drinking habits. He drinks one can of beer almost every day before hitting the sack. In an unexpected turn of events, now I help him chug down what now I think is a nonalcoholic amount and often times we fight over the last can of beer.

On Monday nights, I am regularly reminded of how much beer we and majority of the Japanese population consume. When I shamefully take out our recycling bag close to midnight, deliberately avoiding nosy neighbors, the sizable plastic container shared by the entire street is already largely filled to the brim with empty Asahi cans.

Next to the tranquil Shonai River in the Moriyama Ward, there stands what looks like humongous 500 milliliter beer cans. In reality, or sobriety rather, those cans are the breweries of Asahi. The factory offers tours in English and Japanese that show the complete brewing process from barley to beer. The tours are free of charge and even comes with complimentary glasses of freshly brewed beer.

32. BEER GARDENS

While we're on the subject of beer, let me use this tip to share a number of places where you can drink outdoors and have fun. In a warm and sunny country like the Philippines, drinking alfresco is the norm. Popular drinking spots would typically have a common

Leira Matubis

open area. Just recently my friends and I had a picnic on the side of a mountainous cliff overlooking the city lights below. Here in Japan though, it's quite the contrary. The city is well endowed with indoor pubs, clubs and izakayas but there's nothing quite like the combo of beer and fresh air.

Beer Gardens are all over Sakae and the Meieki area. They are usually alfresco on the rooftops of major buildings, perfect for whiling away warm nights with a few close friends. Some are open anytime of the year, some only in the summer. In Sakae alone, there are 3 beer gardens that I know. One on the rooftop of Mitsukoshi, another on the rooftop of Chunichi Building and another underneath the Nagoya TV Tower. All of which are within a 5-minute walk of each other.

The second best thing about Beer Garden, the first it being alfresco, is the reasonable price. For an average price of 3000 yen, you can choose from a lineup of local and imported beers and a selection of mostly fried food. Business hours vary from garden to garden, normally opening an hour before dusk to let customers enjoy the setting sun with a glass of refreshing beer.

>TOURIST

33. NAGOYA SOUL FOOD

Nagoya is widely believed to be the very home of Japanese soul food. Nagoyans have vamped both Japanese and international favorites, adding their own signature cuisine turning food into mouth-watering variants. The most interesting and tastiest culinary wonders are concocted in Nagoya.

At the very top of Nagoya delicacies is tebasaki. A unique Japanese version of the western buffalo wings, this Nagoya specialty is very hard to forget. This twice-fried crispy goodness is a great match for beer or sake. Tebasaki has a distinct sweet and salty taste with varying degrees of spiciness. Nagoyans have long mastered the art of eating these chicken wings in one powerful swoop, while pulling away the bones. The best tebasaki restaurant is highly debated among locals, the majority split between Furai-bo and Yama-chan.

There's a common joke in Japan that says Nagoyans will put miso in anything. Needless to say, it's nearly impossible to find a person born-and-bred in Nagoya who doesn't like miso, especially the red variant. There are various dishes that incorporate the favored red miso, the most common being Miso Katsu. The crispy pork cutlet is drizzled with a thick sweet-and-salty miso sauce with a distinctly rich flavor of red beans. Many restaurants in Nagoya serve this as a lunch special but the best is Miso-katsu Yabaton.

Another signature dish in Nagoya cuisine is Hitsumabushi or grilled eel. This different method of cooking eel was developed in the highest eel-producing area of Aichi. The term 'hitsumabushi' was coined by Atsuta Horaiken, one of the oldest and most notable restaurants in Nagoya. A time-honored way of how to eat hitsumabushi, faithfully followed by many locals, especially good for first timers, is unique to this area. The serving of eel is divided into four portions, the first eaten plainly; the second eaten with your choice of condiments like wasabi, onions, nori, radish; the third eaten similar to the second portion but with the added tang of broth or green tea; and the last portion eaten the way you liked it best.

34. FOOD FROM THE BASEMENT

The tip doesn't sound as enticing as I had hoped but if you're looking for good, high-quality chow, you'll find it in the basement of many department stores. The B1 food hall in Mitsukoshi in Sakae for instance, is my go-to place for lunch-slash-dinner when I'm at work.

\>TOURIST

Although it obviously costs more given that it's inside a huge establishment, it's so much better than konbini food.

My personal favorite which I had discovered by accident is the underground food hall in JR Takashimaya in Nagoya Station. I couldn't find where to buy a commuter card one day so I bravely asked a station officer in Japanese. All I caught from his response riddled with courteous language was shita meaning 'down' so I took the first flight of stairs I saw and there it was.

An exquisite floor teeming with glass displays boasting mouth-watering food, and friendly Japanese vendors handing out samples of their best sellers. Every Sunday afternoon, I can be found here either buying Pao Pao for dinner or Harbs for dessert. After the miraculous chance discovery of these food paradises, I can say I will never go back to konbini food.

Depachika, as it is known in Japanese, is a definite must-try and must-see. There are very few posts on the internet about depachikas in Nagoya and locals tend to forget easily because they are just something ordinary here. Still I highly recommend it to anyone, whether you just want to grab some food, or you like to splurge on ornately wrapped souvenirs or just admire the general splendor of the basement.

35. NAGASHIMA SPALAND

In May of 2017, the whole family visited me in Nagoya. It was spring so she looked forward to seeing the cherry blossoms for a memorable 50th birthday. Although a reasonable request, the only problem was the trip was scheduled after blooming season, and by then there would be no trace left of cherry blossoms.

Obviously, she was devastated so we started brainstorming other possible highlights. I was throwing a few suggestions in the mix, like Osaka or Kyoto but she insisted on staying within the Greater Nagoya area. So I took them to the equivalent of Disneyland and Universal Studios in Nagoya, the Nagashima Spaland.

I know what you're thinking but no. It isn't a land of Shiatsu massages or hot stone treatments. Rather, it's a magical place full of thrill rides, rolling gears and excited screams. Located in the neighboring Mie prefecture one hour away from Nagoya, Nagashima Spaland has no shortage of fun. With a growing variety of rides, this place is surely for everyone.

>TOURIST

There are many routes you can take going to Nagashima Spaland. So far the best is, you guessed it, by bus. The Meitetsu Bus Center at Nagoya Station offers package tickets for the return trip fare, unlimited rides and small discounts in the adjacent shopping complex. Meitetsu buses travel to Nagashima Spaland on a daily basis with one bus leaving every hour starting as early as 8 o'clock.

36. STEEL DRAGON

Nagashima Spaland's main attraction is the Steel Dragon 2000. With a height of 318 feet and a length of 8,133 feet, it will catch your attention from miles away. The Steel Dragon is THE (emphasis needed) longest steel coaster and one of the 7 only giga coasters in the world. With 2 seats in a row, my sister and I had planned on sitting together but my brother was so terrified we couldn't leave him alone. He screamed like a little girl, poor 20-year-old boy.

Opened in 2000, the year of the dragon, the entire ride lasts for a crazy 4 minutes with the first drop at 307 feet and a speed of 95 mph. On the maddeningly slow initial ascent, I waved to my mom who was carelessly lounged on a park bench. Of course she didn't see me, until now I'm not sure if it was her I was waving to but up at its highest point, she was no bigger than my thumb.

Probably the scariest 4 minutes of my brother's life, the Steel Dragon will make even adrenaline junkies crawl back with their tails behind their legs. After that ride, my brother decided not to go on anymore rides and to join my mother on the park bench.

37. WHITE CYCLONE

One of the oldest wooden roller coasters in the world is also in Nagashima Spaland. From afar, the White Cyclone looks like flawless snow-covered mountains but when you look at the white wooden beams up close, it's an architectural marvel.

Built in 1994 and operated since the park's opening, White Cyclone still uses original frames entirely out of sturdy Alaskan timber. Its age has become its selling point with most riders tuning in on the squeaks and screeches of the elderly coaster. The White Cyclone has long been a symbol of the park, apart from its younger brother the Steel Dragon and the humongous air-conditioned Aurora Wheel.

>TOURIST

As the name suggests, the White Cyclone is definitely a bumpy ride. Complete with bunny hills, spiraling tracks and tunneled trails, it surely feels like you're trapped in the eye of a tropical storm. The cars are, as you would expect, old but completely safe except for the turbulence which left us with sore arms and bottoms.

Sadly, you won't have to worry about sore bottoms anymore. The White Cyclone ran for the last time just a few months ago in January of 2018. The park has decided to refurbish it and make a new hybrid coaster of wood and steel scheduled to start operations in 2019. Nonetheless, the perpetual roller coaster legend is still is a sight to see, definitely worth a couple of instagrams.

38. JAZZ DREAM

If you are a shopaholic looking to satisfy your cravings, this is the mall for you. Jazz Dream is one of the biggest outlet malls in Japan. It boasts an impressive selection of over 200 world renowned and Japanese brands. You won't leave this place without a few shopping bags.

Leira Matubis

Officially known as Mitsui Outlet Park, Jazz Dream is a shopper's paradise. Boasting names from far across the world like Coach, Dolce & Gabbana, Givenchy and Armani; sporting goods like Nike, Puma, Reebok; and local brands like United Arrows, Ships and Tomorrowland at highly discounted prices, it's a challenge to keep your wallet closed.

Located right next to Nagashima Spaland, it's the best place to go after an exhilarating day at the park. There is wide range of restaurants to choose from and there are outdoor seats where you can hang out and relax. The outlet has two huge food courts where you can indulge in an affordable lineup of international and Japanese cuisine. The entire area is designed to resemble the streets of the French Quarter in New Orleans, with Jazz music blasting through the network of speakers complete the atmosphere of the place.

39. NABANA NO SATO

A great side trip when you decide to visit Nagashima SpaLand is Nabana no Sato. Although located at considerable 15 minutes by bus away from the other attractions, this picture perfect garden is another stop in this trip to Nagashima. This flower park overflows with

>TOURIST

an impressive collection of 12,000 different species of flowers.

Nabana no Sato can be visited any time of the day, any time of the year. Viewing their flower gardens are best done in the daytime when the sun supplies them with its nutritious light. Expertly cultivated flowers are displayed in their huge greenhouse every year. Each season, they showcase flowers in bloom like tulips, hydrangeas and irises in the spring and dahlias in the autumn.

To see an aerial view of the park, take a ride on Island Fuji, a moving observatory, and bask on the glorious landscape. If it gets too hot, there are restaurants and a beer garden where you can enjoy a cold pint. If your feet start aching from strolling the vast park, head to the foot spa and take a quick relaxing break. On your way out, you can also buy potted plants and freshly picked flowers at the flower market right outside.

40. WINTER ILLUMINATION

Winter Illuminations are such huge things in Japan that in every prefecture, there is one. Some small scale and modest like street lights, some moderate in size like

Leira Matubis

tall buildings and towers, and some incredibly large like thousands of square meters of land.

In the Greater Nagoya area, Nabana no Sato hosts one of the most beautiful illuminations. It's safe to say they don't hold back when it comes to led lights. Using around 8 million led lights, the parks are illuminated to depict different beautiful scenes from all over the world. To name a few, they have already exhibited Mount Fuji, the Swiss Alps and the Northern Lights in the past. Last year in 2017, they decided on Kumamon as the theme of the show. The cute mascot hails from Kumamoto Prefecture, which suffered a huge blow after the powerful earthquake of 2016.

The most visited part of the whole park is the famous light tunnel. The 200-meter light tunnel attracts an unbelievable number of people every year. Just recently, a new tunnel was added to the vast attractions. The Kawazu Sakura tunnel is a smaller and shorter version of its predecessor. Illuminated with pink lights, it looks just like lounging below cherry trees in full bloom in the spring.

>TOURIST

41. YUAMI NO SHIMA

Because of the many things to see in this little island of Nagashima, many will say one day isn't enough for these attractions clumped together. If you really want to be able to visit everything, it would be preferable to stay here at least one night. Conveniently, there is a hotel within the huge complex.

Just around the corner, there is an onsen resort called Yuami no Shima. It has 17 different kinds of outdoor and indoor baths, great for whiling the night away after an exhausting day of roller coasters, shopping and light shows. Bathing in geothermal goodness while viewing magnificent natural scenery is a memorably unique experience

In the past when there was little medical technology, the Japanese people dipped in onsens to cure injures and heal ailments. Because the country is volcanically active, there are thousands of natural hot springs scattered around. Now onsens are a past time for locals and a point of interest for many visitors.

Just like its original purpose, soaking in the tranquil hot water and admiring the beautiful views Yuami no Shima definitely has miraculous power of relieving stress or at least, making you forget temporarily. Apart from the beautiful outdoor baths, the onsen complex also has saunas and spas to boot.

42. NAGOYA SWEETS AND SNACKS

Of course any cuisine culture wouldn't be complete without afternoon snacks and scrumptious sweets. There's always a restaurant, a coffee shop, a souvenir store or a kombini in sight that serves specialty snacks and desserts. There's never a shortage of sugar and red miso in Nagoya.

The cutest by far is Pyorin which is only sold in Cafe Gentiane in Nagoya Station. This adorable dessert is a normal custard pudding covered in vanilla mousse and decorated with chips of chocolate. What makes Pyorin unique to Nagoya is the main ingredient, eggs from Kochin chickens. These prime quality and pure-bred poultry are the inspiration behind the catchy Pyorin look.

Another cherished favorite is Nagoya's version of the western peanut butter and jelly combo. Known as Ogura-an, it is thick toast topped a hefty serving of red bean paste with butter. This tasty treat is sold in many coffee shops, usually as part of the breakfast menu.

>TOURIST

Komeda Coffee, a large cafe chain, serves this breakfast special with the red bean paste and margarine on the side so it can be eaten according to preference.

Nagoya also has its own special version of the Japanese staple, onigiri or rice balls. This simple snack, called tenmusu, is a rice ball stuffed with shrimp tempura. The tempura tips peek from the top and are secured by nori or sheets of dried seaweed. Unlike original onigiri seasoned with salt, tenmusu is plain and simple, relying on the shrimp and nori for taste. A popular takeout snack, tenmusu can be bought in nearly all convenient stores but can also be enjoyed in some restaurants. A traditional restaurant in the Osu Shopping district called Senju is well known as the restaurant that serves the best tenmusu in Nagoya.

43. FLUFFY PANCAKES

Now I'm sure you've read, seen or heard about the thick fluffy pancakes in Japan somewhere on the internet. I salivated at a trending video one time when I still lived in the Philippines, I just knew I had to try it. There are many restaurants that offer these pancakes but the best I've tried so far is from Hoshino.

Leira Matubis

Hoshino is a chain of coffee shops that have plastic displays outfront to help foreign customers make an informed order. Scattered around the city, the cozy cafes offer a variety of hand-dripped coffee, original desserts and house recipe pastas. Their best seller, as you may have guessed, is their soufflé pancakes.

An interesting twist to the customary flat ones, the pancakes jiggled and swayed with the movement as the waiter delivered it to my table. I don't remember how many photos in how many different angles I took before taking that first bite. Even without the syrup and the butter, the distinct airy texture and eggy taste is refreshing.

The only problem with Hoshino is that their accessible branches are almost always full during peak times. For one, there's a Hoshino in the Sakae Underground less than 5 minutes from my office building. I normally get 80-minute breaks during lunch but not once have I eaten there without falling in line. The best time to sample their divinely soft pancakes is in the quiet time before 11AM and after 2PM.

>TOURIST

44. CURRY PAN

Curry pan is a Japanese household favorite. The deep-fried, panko-covered goodness is filled with a stew of tender meat, potatoes and carrots enhanced by spices and herbs with a flavorful aroma. Curry pan can be found anywhere from konbinis to supermarkets to specially dedicated bakeries. It is also my personal favorite out of all the commonly sold assortments of bread in Japan.

Whenever I walk into a bakery, curry pan is the first thing I look for. My boyfriend has given me the stink eye multiple times because he can't understand why I like curry better with bread than with rice. After having discovered and tried many places, I've narrowed down my favorites to two bakeries in Nagoya Station.

The first bakery is right before the wickets of the Aonami Line. I had long ignored this small unassuming bakery for the adjacent McDonald's but I admit the oversight on my part. On some Saturdays, I would hurriedly grab a McMuffin from McDonald's on the way to work but one day there was an unexpectedly long line. I entered the intimate bakery next to it, fittingly named Little Mermaid. Frankly, their selection of bread wasn't quite inviting, there wasn't anything

Leira Matubis

that called to me so I without thinking I bought 2 kinds of my favorite curry pan, one plain and one with a soft-boiled egg. The plain one wasn't so special but the soft-boiled egg really kicked it up a notch. The sweetness of the runny yolk balanced the overly-spiced curry. From that day on, my outlook of that small bakery changed. Needless to say, the staff now know me as the curry pan maniac.

The other bakery is in Gate Walk, a few minutes from the entrance of the Higashiyama Line which I also use on a daily basis. The name of the bakery, Cascade, doesn't make much sense but it's twice the size of Little Mermaid. It also has twice as many customers and twice as many varieties. Additionally unlike Little Mermaid, Cascade crafts very appealing desserts and bread. It has about 5 different kinds of curry pan which, of course, I have tried. My absolute favorite is their plain curry pan which is distinct because it's coated with a different kind of panko making the crust crunchier and more explosive. Their curry is a little more seasoned than others but the extra crunch complements it well.

These two bakeries sound like polar opposites but disturbingly, they have one similarity. Cascade is also next to McDonald's. Coincidence? Maybe not.

>TOURIST

45. ROUND ONE AND SPOCHA

Round one is a multi-level arcade filled with all kinds of entertainment mashed together in one complex. Many teenagers spend their afternoons here before going to cram school. It is a place to kill boredom and misery and instead feel bitterness because the crane machines are impossible to beat.

Upon entering the first floor, rows and rows and rows of slot, crane and betting machines are there for your displeasure. Up on the second floor, faint, scratchy, off-key and occasionally in-tune voices permeate the supposedly soundproof karaoke rooms but these floors aren't where you want to stay. Grab your tickets, pay your fees quickly. You don't want to get sucked into this inescapable black hole that is a pachinko parlor. Go up to Spocha on the 3rd and 4th floor because that's where the real fun is at.

My boyfriend took me here once on an unplanned date. I was extremely dismayed because of my chronic tardiness so he decided to cheer me up by getting tickets to an arcade complex 15 minutes away from where we live. We see the huge bowling pin every day and we pass it everytime we go grocery shopping in the supermarket beside it. Sounds pathetic because we're fully grown adults but frankly, it was the most fun I've ever had in a long time.

Must-tries in Spocha are the Segway rink and augmented reality games on the 3rd floor; and the Zorb ball, batting areas and hoverboards on the 4th floor. There are many interesting games like table tennis, tennis, rodeos, volleyball, basketball, mini-golf and gun ranges. There are also massage chairs, a reading area and a snack bar for the kill-joys.

46. PORT OF NAGOYA PUBLIC AQUARIUM

First opened in 1992 and located near Nagoya-ko Station on the Meijo Line, the Port of Nagoya Public Aquarium exhibits marine life and environment in five different aquatic regions, namely Japanese, Australian, the Antarctic, equatorial and tropical. There are two main buildings, the North and South, that accommodate different kinds of sea animals.

In the North building, a few different kinds of media are used to narrate the long history of marine life. Large tanks with bottlenose dolphins, orcas and belugas represent how intelligent sea mammals are to have adjusted to living in the constantly changing oceans.

>TOURIST

The Main Pool on the top floor where performances are held can seat an audience of 3000 people. On the open tanks, visitors can witness feeding or training dolphins. On some occasions, trainers allow curious kids to pet the friendly dolphins.

A different theme dominates the South building. Visitors are pulled into a marine journey starting from Japanese waters all the way to the Antarctic. Crawlies and creatures are the leading attraction here and the aquarium shows how smaller animals and organisms have adapted to different aquatic environments. Giant crabs, half-buried worms, multicolor fish, sea turtles and penguins live in recreated habitats.

The last room before you exit the South Building is the touch tank. As the name suggests, children and adults can touch and hold many kinds of small marine life such as starfish and shell fish. A trip here will definitely be a fun and information filled day for the whole family.

47. LEGOLAND

Legoland is a recently opened attraction here in Nagoya. Despite the odd choice of location, in the middle of the industrial district of Nagoya, the almost

Leira Matubis

one year old theme park has already attracted an impressive number of visitors. Since its opening, Legoland has received a mixed number of reviews from people.

After some research, I've concluded that Legoland really is a place for young children. The many rides, games and play areas around the park are aimed at young kids while teenagers and adults are not likely to find something they enjoy except for the stunning lego sculptures scattered around the park.

Inside, there are 7 themed areas that uses millions and millions of lego blocks. In Miniland, there are recreations of Tokyo Station, Kiyomizu Temple in Kyoto, Nagoya Castle and Mount Fuji great for a quick photo-op. There are many fun and exciting experiences for kids in Lego City such as learning how to drive lego cars, training to become a coast guard and putting out a burning building.

I personally thought the ticket prices were too high for a relatively small theme park. The prices were close to Tokyo Disneyland and Universal Studios Japan which I felt was steep for a theme park you can cover in less than a few hours. As you can imagine, theme parks tend to get crowded on peak days so visiting on the weekdays is preferable.

>TOURIST

Like mentioned above, it doesn't take a whole day to cover the entire park. Adjacent to Legoland, a new aquarium and a hotel is scheduled to open in 2018. Aside from that, a commercial complex sits right outside and opened around the same time as Legoland. Known as Maker's Pier, the complex has a number of interesting lifestyle shops and restaurants. Also in the nearby area is Port Messe, officially called Nagoya International Exhibition Hall. They hold different events like trade shows, flea markets, garden fairs, bike shows and more. Checking out Maker's Pier and Port Messe will definitely make great side trips to to a day at Legoland.

48. SCMAGLEV AND RAILWAY PARK

Another attraction in the Kinjo-futo area is SCMAGLEV and Railway Park owned by the main operating railway company in Aichi, JR Central. The park exhibits old and new trains where visitors can really learn a lot about an integral part of daily life that are normally taken for granted, trains and railways.

The SCMAGLEV and Railway Park has a permanent exhibit of 39 full-length trains including steam locomotives, electric cars, conventional lines, bullet trains and the sleek new SC Maglev. An incredible diorama, complete with moving trains, is also on permanent display. The accurate and incredibly detailed miniaturization of the surrounding areas on the Tokaido Shinkansen line is one of the largest train dioramas in Japan.

The entire park takes visitors to a whole new experience, providing a deeper understanding and learning of railway systems. There are rooms on the side of the rolling stock exhibit that lets lucky visitors try their hand at driving Shinkansens and conventional lines through simulation games. Visitors have the choice to rent a touchscreen device similar to an iPad that works as a tour guide. It has a user-friendly interface and provides simple explanations of rolling stock highlights using both audio and visual aids in a number different languages. Kids are free to explore, discover, roam around and enter the different cars to see what's inside.

49. NAGOYA SOUVENIRS

Since Nagoya is home to some very interesting icons and varieties of food, the selection of souvenirs is a refreshing array of knick knacks. For cookies, crackers and other snacks, Nagoya Station would be the best place for one-stop souvenir shopping.

The basement food hall in Takashimaya sells souvenirs in nicely packed boxes perfect for giving to family, friends or coworkers. For a cheaper alternative, numerous gift kiosks and convenient stores can be found anywhere from train platforms, near wickets and near the Shinkansen entrances. These stores are extremely noticeable as some staff would stand outside holding promotions or loudly announcing new products.

Many confectionary and snack companies have incorporated the special Nagoya delicacies in their line up of products like cookies, chips, chocolates and candy. KitKat and the crispy Langue de Chat cookies are the most popular among the ogura-flavored selection. For tebasaki, there's Chipstar and Calbee Jagariko.

Uiro-mochi is another famous choice for sweet traditional souvenirs. It's a Japanese steamed cake made of rice flour. The consistency is thicker and chewier than jelly but it has a smooth texture. Uiro is a very pretty gift, come in different colors depending on the flavor. The most common are red bean, matcha, strawberry, chestnut and yuzu, a citrus fruit.

As I already mentioned, for samurai and kinshachi goods and other Nagoya items can be bought in Nagoya Castle. Buy everything you need before you leave because it's hard to find other souvenir shops in the city that specialize in Nagoya-specific memorabilia but generic Japan knicknacks can all be found in Osu Kannon, Sakae or Kanayama. Don Quixote, a popular discount chain known for its blue penguin logo, is a supermarket, pharmacy, clothing, electronics, appliance, toy, and cosmetic store all rolled into one. Daiso in the Skyle Building is a great place to buy benri goods or life hack items, adorable stationery for kids or anything you need at a low price. Village Vanguard, inside Parco, is for those who love popular Japanese subcultures. This playground themed store is teeming with all kinds of comics, books, toys, keychains, even rare Japanese snacks and imported sodas.

>TOURIST

50. OTHER SPOTS AND NEIGHBORING PLACES

If you're planning to visit Nagoya and have done your research, I'm sure you've already realized that this is not (yet) a comprehensive travel guide as I have omitted, several well-known points of interest from the list. To clarify, that decision was made not because I think lowly of these places, but because I wanted to make space for others that do not receive as much attention on the internet or otherwise. In this last tip, let me mention these prominent areas that will complete your trip.

The Nagoya TV Tower, Oasis 21, Central Park, Sunshine Sakae, Sakae Underground and Otsu Dori are all worth a visit. In Meieki, the Sky Promenade in Midland Square is also widely visited for the panoramic view of Nagoya's skyline and gourmet cuisine. The Tsurumai Park, Shirakawa Park, Higashiyama Park and Yamazaki River are the top places for cherry blossom viewing. The Yamazaki Mazak Museum of Art, Nagoya/Boston Museum of Fine Arts, The Showa Museum of Art, Aichi Prefectural Museum and International Design Center are other great museums.

Leira Matubis

Outside of Nagoya, there are many places to visit that will make for great side trips or day trips. Inuyama Castle, Arimatsu Town, Meiji Mura, Shirakawa Village, Iwasaki Castle, Toyokawa Inari Shrine, Korankei Valley, Tokoname Pottery Town and Toyota Automobile Museum are all easily accessible from the city.

>TOURIST

TOP REASONS TO BOOK THIS TRIP

Food: The unique cuisine is one of Nagoya's trademarks. Best known as Nagoyameshi, the food is well loved by locals although strongly disliked by other Japanese. Marked by a blend of sweetness, saltiness and spice and complemented by locally grown specialties, authentic Nagoyameshi cannot be tasted anywhere else.

Records: Nagoya boasts many records in Japan and in the world. Home to the second biggest planetarium in the world, two of the largest shrines in Japan, the longest and one of the tallest steel coasters in the world, the world's most handsome gorilla and more, Nagoya is definitely a trip that's one for the books.

Authenticity: The equal balance of traditional and modern lifestyles in Nagoya make for an authentic Japan experience. Unlike overwhelmingly large cities, Nagoya gives you room to breathe and let everything sink in. There's a great deal of history and advancement of Japan that roots from Nagoya. The city will bring you back to the past, into the future and deeper into the present.

Leira Matubis

>TOURIST

Bonus Book

50 THINGS TO KNOW ABOUT PACKING LIGHT FOR TRAVEL

Pack the Right Way Every Time

Author: Manidipa Bhattacharyya

Leira Matubis

First Published in 2015 by Dr. Lisa Rusczyk. Copyright 2015. All Rights Reserved. No part of this publication may be reproduced, including scanning and photocopying, or distributed in any form or by any means, electronic or mechanical, or stored in a database or retrieval system without prior written permission from the publisher.

Disclaimer: The publisher has put forth an effort in preparing and arranging this book. The information provided herein by the author is provided "as is". Use this information at your own risk. The publisher is not a licensed doctor. Consult your doctor before engaging in any medical activities. The publisher and author disclaim any liabilities for any loss of profit or commercial or personal damages resulting from the information contained in this book.

Edited by Melanie Howthorne

Introduction

He who would travel happily must travel light.

-Antoine de Saint-Exupéry

Travel takes you to different places from seas and mountains to deserts and much more. In your travels you get to interact with different people and their cultures. You will, however, enjoy the sights and interact positively with these new people even more, if you are travelling light.

When you travel light your mind can be free from worry about your belongings. You do not have to spend precious vacation time waiting for your luggage to arrive after a long flight. There is be no chance of your bags going missing and the best part is that you need not pay a fee for checked baggage.

People who have mastered this art of packing light will root for you to take only one carry-on, wherever you go. However, many people can find it really hard to pack light. More so if you are travelling with children. Differentiating between "must have" and "just in case" items is the starting point. There will be ample shopping avenues at your destination which are just

Leira Matubis

waiting to be explored, take the chance, go shopping at a new market.

This book will show you 'packing' in a new 'light' – pun intended – and help you to embrace light packing practices for all of your future travels.

Off to packing!

Dedication

I dedicate this book to all the travel buffs that I know, who have given me great insights into the contents of their backpacks.

About The Author

Manidipa Bhattacharyya is a creative writer and editor, with an education in English literature and Linguistics. After working in the IT industry for seven long years she decided to call it quits and follow her heart instead. Manidipa has been ghost writing, editing, proof reading and doing secondary research services for many story tellers and article writers for about three years. She stays in Kolkata, India with her husband and a busy two year old. In her own time Manidipa enjoys travelling, photography and writing flash fiction.

Manidipa believes in travelling light and never carries anything that she couldn't haul herself on a trip. However, travelling with her child changed the scenario. She seemed to carry the entire world with her for the baby on the first two trips. But good sense prevailed and she is again working her way to becomming a light traveller, this time with a kid.

Leira Matubis

>TOURIST

The Right Travel Gear
1. Choose Your Travel Gear Carefully

While selecting your travel gear, pick items that are light weight, durable and most importantly, easy to carry. There are cases with wheels so you can drag them along – these are usually on the heavy side because of the trolley. Alternatively a backpack that you can carry comfortably on your back, or even a duffel bag that you can carry easily by hand or sling across your body are also great options. Whatever you choose, one thing to keep in mind is that the luggage itself should not weigh a ton, this will give you the flexibility to bring along one extra pair of shoes if you so desire.

2. Carry The Minimum Number Of Bags

Selecting light weight luggage is not everything. You need to restrict the number of bags you carry as well. One carry-on size bag is ideal for light travel. Most carriers allow one cabin baggage plus one purse, handbag or camera bag as long as it slides under the seat in front. So technically, you can carry two items of luggage without checking them in.

3. Pack One Extra Bag

Always pack one extra empty bag along with your essential items. This could be a very light weight duffel bag or even a sturdy tote bag which takes up minimal space. In the event that you end up buying a lot of souvenirs, you already have a handy bag to stuff all that into and do not have to spend time hunting for an appropriate bag.

> *I'm very strict with my packing and have everything in its right place. I never change a rule. I hardly use anything in the hotel room. I wheel my own wardrobe in and that's it.*
>
> Charlie Watts

Clothes & Accessories
4. Plan Ahead

Figure out in advance what you plan to do on your trip. That will help you to pick that one dress you need for the occasion. If you are going to attend a wedding then you have to carry formal wear. If not, you can ditch the gown for something lighter that will be comfortable during long walks or on the beach.

5. Wear That Jacket

Remember that wearing items will not add extra luggage for your air travel. So wear that bulky jacket that you plan to carry for your trip. This saves space and can also help keep you warm during the chilly flight.

6. Mix and Match

Carry clothes that can be interchangeably used to reinvent your look. Find one top that goes well with a couple of pairs of pants or skirts. Use tops, shirts and jackets wisely along with other accessories like a scarf or a stole to create a new look.

7. Choose Your Fabric Wisely

Stuffing clothes in cramped bags definitely takes its toll which results in wrinkles. It is best to carry wrinkle free, synthetic clothes or merino tops. This will eliminate the need for that small iron you usually bring along.

8. Ditch Clothes Pack Underwear

Pack more underwear and socks. These are the things that will give you a fresh feel even if you do not get a chance to wear fresh clothes. Moreover these are easy to wash and can be dried inside the hotel room itself.

9. Choose Dark Over Light

While picking your clothes choose dark coloured ones. They are easy to colour coordinate and can last longer before needing a wash. Accidental food spills and dirt from the road are less visible on darker clothes.

10. Wear Your Jeans

Take only one pair of Jeans with you, which you should wear on the flight. Remember to pick a pair that can be worn for sightseeing trips and is equally eloquent for

>TOURIST

dinner. You can add variety by adding light weight cargoes and chinos.

11. Carry Smart Accessories

The right accessory can give you a fresh look even with the same old dress. An intelligent neck-piece, a couple of bright scarves, stoles or a sarong can be used in a number of ways to add variety to your clothing. These light weight beauties can double up as a nursing cover, a light blanket, beach wear, a modesty cover for visiting places of worship, and also makes for an enthralling game of peek-a-boo.

12. Learn To Fold Your Garments

Seasoned travellers all swear by rolling their clothes for compact and wrinkle free packing. Bundle packing, where you roll the clothes around a central object as if tying it up, is also a popular method of compact and wrinkle free packing. Stacking folded clothes one on top of another is a big no-no as it makes creases extreme and they are difficult to get rid of without ironing.

13. Wash Your Dirty Laundry

One of the ways to avoid carrying loads of clothes is to wash the clothes you carry. At some places you might get to use the laundry services or a Laundromat but if you are in a pinch, best solution is to wash them yourself. If that is the plan then carrying quick drying clothes is highly recommended, which most often also happen to be the wrinkle free variety.

14. Leave Those Towels Behind

Regular towels take up a lot of space, are heavy and take ages to dry out. If you are staying at hotels they will provide you with towels anyway. If you are travelling to a remote place, where the availability of towels look doubtful, carry a light weight travel towel of viscose material to do the job.

15. Use A Compression Bag

Compression bags are getting lots of recommendation now days from regular travellers. These are useful for saving space in your luggage when you have to pack bulky dresses. While packing for the return trip, get help from the hotel staff to arrange a vacuum cleaner.

Footwear

16. Put On Your Hiking Boots

If you have plans to go hiking or trekking during your trip, you will need those bulky hiking boots. The best way to carry them is to wear them on flight to save space and luggage weight. You can remove the boots once inside and be comfortable in your socks.

17. Picking The Right Shoes

Shoes are often the bulkiest items, along with being the dainty if you are a female. They need care and take up a lot of space in your luggage. It is advisable therefore to pick shoes very carefully. If you plan to do a lot of walking and site seeing, then wearing a pair of comfortable walking shoes are a must. For more formal occasions you can carry durable, light weight flats which will not take up much space.

18. Stuff Shoes

If you happen to pack a pair of shoes, ensure you utilize their hollow insides. Tuck small items like rolled up socks or belts to save space. They will also be easy to find.

Toiletries
19. Stashing Toiletries

Carry only absolute necessities. Airline rules dictate that for one carry-on bag, liquids and gels must be in 3.4 ounce (100ml) bottles or less, and must be packed in a one quart zip-lock bag. If you are planning to stay in a hotel, the basic things will be provided for you. It's best is to buy the rest from the local market at your destination.

20. Take Along Tampons

Tampons are a hard to find item in a lot of countries. Figure out how many you need and pack accordingly. For longer stays you can buy them online and have them delivered to where you are staying.

21. Get Pampered Before You Travel

Some avid travellers suggest getting a pedicure and manicure just the day before travelling. This not only gives you a well kept look, you also save the trouble of packing nail polish. Remember, every little bit of weight reduced adds up.

Electronics
22. Lugging Along Electronics

Electronics have a large role to play in our lives today. Most of us cannot imagine our lives away from our phones, laptops or tablets. However while travelling, one must consider the amount of weight these electronics add to our luggage. Thankfully smart phones come along with all the essentials tools like a camera, email access, picture editing tools and more. They are smart to the point of eliminating the need to carry multiple gadgets. Choose a smart phone that suits all your requirements and travel with the world in your palms or pocket.

23. Reduce The Number Of Chargers

If you do travel with multiple electronic devices, you will have to bear the additional burden of carrying all their chargers too. Check if a single charger can be used for multiple devices. You might also consider investing in a pocket charger. These small devices support multiple devices while keeping you charged on the go.

Leira Matubis

24. Travel Friendly Apps

Along with smart phones come numerous apps, which are immensely helpful in our travels. You name it and you have an app for it at hand – take pictures, sharing with friends and family, torch to light dark roads, maps, checking flight/train times, find hotels and many other things. Use these smart alternatives to traditional items like books to eliminate weight and save space.

I get ideas about what's essential when packing my suitcase.

-Diane von Furstenberg

Travelling With Kids
25. Bring Along The Stroller

Kids might enjoy walking for while but they soon tire out and a stroller is the just the right thing for them to rest in while you continue your tour. Strollers also double duty as a luggage carrier and shopping bag holder. Remember to pick a light weight, easy to handle brand of stroller. Better yet, find out in advance if you can rent a stroller at your destination.

26. Bring Only Enough Diapers For Your Trip

Diapers take up a lot of space and add to the weight of your luggage. Therefore it is advisable to carry just enough diapers to last through the trip and a few for afterwards, till you buy fresh stock at your destination. Unless of course you are travelling to a really remote area, in which case you have no choice but to carry the load. Otherwise diapers are something you will find pretty easily.

27. Take Only A Couple Of Toys

Children are easily attracted by new things in their environment. While travelling they will find numerous 'new' objects to scrutinize and play with. Packing just one favourite toy is enough, or if there is no favourite toy leave out all of them in favour of stories or imaginary games.

28. Carry Kid Friendly Snacks

Create a small snack counter in your bag to store away quick bites for those sudden hunger pangs. Depending on the child's age this could include chocolates, raisins, dry fruits, granola bars or biscuits. Also keep a bottle of water handy for your little one. These things do not add much weight and can be adjusted in a handbag or knapsack.

29. Games To Carry

Create some travel specific, imaginary games if you have slightly grown up children, like spot the attractions. Keep a colouring book and colours handy for in-flight or hotel time. Apps on your smart phone can keep the children engaged with cartoons and story books. Older children are often entertained by games available on phones or tablets. This cuts the weight of luggage down while keeping the kids entertained.

30. Let The Kids Carry Their Load

A good thing is to start early sharing of responsibilities. Let your child pick a bag of his or her choice and pack it themselves. Keep tabs on what they are stuffing in their bags by asking if they will be using that item on the trip. It could start out being just an entertainment bag initially but with growing years they will learn to sort the useful from the superfluous. Children as little as four can maneuver a small trolley suitcase like a pro- their experience in pull along toys credit.

31. Decide on Location for Children to Sleep

While on a trip you might not always get a crib at your destination, and carrying one will make life all the more difficult. Instead call ahead to see if there are any cribs or roll out beds for children. You may even put blankets on the floor. Weave them a story about camping and they will gladly sleep without any trouble.

32. Get Baby Products Delivered At Your Destination

If you are absolutely paranoid about not getting your favourite variety of diaper or brand of baby food, check out online stores like amazon.com for services in your destination city. You can buy things online ahead of your travel and get them delivered to your hotel upon arrival.

33. Feeding Needs Of Your Infants

If you are travelling with a breastfed infant, you save the trouble of carrying bottles and bottle sanitization kits. For special food, or medications, you may need to call ahead to make sure you have a refrigerator where you are staying.

34. Feeding Needs Of Your Toddler

With the progression from infancy to toddler, their dietary requirements too evolve. You will have to pack some snacks for travelling time. Fresh fruits and vegetables can be purchased at your destination. Most of the cities you travel to in whichever part of the world, will have baby food products and formulas, available at the local drug-store or the supermarket.

35. Picking Clothes For Your Baby

Contrary to popular belief, babies can do without many changes of clothes. At the most pack 2 outfits per day. Pack mix and match type clothes for your little one as well. Pick things which are comfortable to wear and quick to dry.

36. Selecting Shoes For Your Baby

Like outfits, kids can make do with two pairs of comfortable shoes. If you can get some water resistant shoes it will be best. To expedite drying wet shoes, you can stuff newspaper in them then wrap them with newspaper and leave them to dry overnight.

37. Keep One Change Of Clothes Handy

Travelling with kids can be tricky. Keep a change of clothes for the kids and mum handy in your purse or tote bag. This takes a bit of space in your hand luggage but comes extremely handy in case there are any accidents or spills.

38. Leave Behind Baby Accessories

Baby accessories like their bed, bath tub, car seat, crib etc. should be left at home. Many hotels provide a crib on request, while car seats can be borrowed from friends or rented. Babies can be given a bath in the hotel sink or even in the adult bath tub with a little bit of water. If you bring a few bath toys, they can be used in the bath, pool, and out of water. They can also be sanitized easily in the sink.

39. Carry A Small Load Of Plastic Bags

With children around there are chances of a number of soiled clothes and diapers. These plastic bags help to sort the dirt from the clean inside your big bag. These are very light weight and come in handy to other carry stuff as well at times.

>TOURIST

Pack with a Purpose
40. Packing For Business Trips

One neutral-coloured suit should suffice. It can be paired with different shirts, ties and accessories for different occasions. One pair of black suit pants could be worn with a matching jacket for the office or with a snazzy top for dinner.

41. Packing For A Cruise

Most cruises have formal dinners, and that formal dress usually takes up a lot of space. However you might find a tuxedo to rent. For women, a short black dress with multiple accessory options will do the trick.

42. Packing For A Long Trip Over Different Climates

The secret packing mantra for travel over multiple climates is layering. Layering traps air around your body creating insulation against the cold. The same light t-shirt that is comfortable in a warmer climate can be the innermost layer in a colder climate.

Leira Matubis

Reduce Some More Weight
43. Leave Precious Things At Home

Things that you would hate to lose or get damaged leave them at home. Precious jewellery, expensive gadgets or dresses, could be anything. You will not require these on your trip. Leave them at home and spare the load on your mind.

44. Send The Load Of Souvenirs By Post

If you have spent all your money on purchasing souvenirs, carrying them back in the same bag that you brought along would be difficult. Either pack everything in another bag and check it in the airport or get everything shipped to your home. Use an international carrier for a secure transit, but this could be more expensive than the checking fees at the airport.

45. Avoid Carrying Books

Books equal to weight. There are many reading apps which you can download on your smart phone or tab.

Plus there are gadgets like Kindle and Nook that are thinner and lighter alternatives to your regular book.

Check, Get, Set, Check Again
46. Strategize Before Packing

Create a travel list and prepare all that you think you need to carry along. Keep everything on your bed or floor before packing and then think through once again – do I really need that? Any item that meets this question can be avoided. Remove whatever you don't really need and pack the rest.

47. Test Your Luggage

Once you have fully packed for the trip take a test trip with your luggage. Take your bags and go to town for window shopping for an hour. If you enjoy your hour long trip it is good to go, if not, go home and reduce the load some more. Repeat this test till you hit the right weight.

48. Add A Roll Of Duct Tape

You might wonder why, when this book has been talking about reducing stuff, we're suddenly asking you to pack something totally unusual. This is because when you have limited supplies, duct tape is immensely helpful for small repairs – a broken bag, leaking ziplock bag, broken sunglasses, you name it and duct tape can fix it, temporarily.

49. Our List Of Essential Items

Even though the emphasis is on packing light, there are things which have to be carried for any trip. Here is our list of essentials:

- Passport/Visa or any other ID

- Any other paper work that might be required on a trip like permits, hotel reservation confirmations etc.

- Medicines – all your prescription medicines and emergency kit, especially if you are travelling with children

- Medical or vaccination records

- Money in foreign currency if travelling to a different country

- Tickets- Email or Message them to your phone

>TOURIST

50. Make The Most Of Your Trip

Wherever you are going, whatever you hope to do we encourage you to embrace it wholeheartedly. Take in the scenery, the culture and above all, enjoy your time away from home.

On a long journey even a straw weighs heavy.

-Spanish Proverb

Leira Matubis

Read other Greater Than a Tourist Books

Greater Than a Tourist San Miguel de Allende Guanajuato Mexico:
50 Travel Tips from a Local by Tom Peterson

Greater Than a Tourist – Lake George Area New York USA:
50 Travel Tips from a Local by Janine Hirschklau

Greater Than a Tourist – Monterey California United States:
50 Travel Tips from a Local by Katie Begley

Greater Than a Tourist – Chanai Crete Greece:
50 Travel Tips from a Local by Dimitra Papagrigoraki

Greater Than a Tourist – The Garden Route Western Cape Province South Africa:
50 Travel Tips from a Local by Li-Anne McGregor van Aardt

Greater Than a Tourist – Sevilla Andalusia Spain:
50 Travel Tips from a Local by Gabi Gazon

Greater Than a Tourist – Kota Bharu Kelantan Malaysia:
50 Travel Tips from a Local by Aditi Shukla

Children's Book: Charlie the Cavalier Travels the World by Lisa Rusczyk

Leira Matubis

> TOURIST
GREATER THAN A TOURIST

Visit GreaterThanATourist.com:
http://GreaterThanATourist.com

Sign up for the Greater Than a Tourist Newsletter:
http://eepurl.com/cxspyf

Follow us on Facebook:
https://www.facebook.com/GreaterThanATourist

Follow us on Pinterest:
http://pinterest.com/GreaterThanATourist

Follow us on Instagram:
http://Instagram.com/GreaterThanATourist

Follow on Twitter:
http://twitter.com/ThanaTourist

Leira Matubis

> TOURIST
GREATER THAN A TOURIST

Please leave your honest review of this book on Amazon and Goodreads. Thank you. We appreciate your positive and constructive feedback. Thank you.

Leira Matubis

>TOURIST

NOTES

Made in the USA
Las Vegas, NV
20 May 2024